Words I left unsaid

Sneh Ratna Choudhary

BookLeaf Publishing

India | USA | UK

Presentation by *BookLeaf Publishing*

Web: www.bookleafpub.com

E-mail: info@bookleafpub.com

ISBN: 9789363316720

First edition 2024

Presentation by *BookLeaf Publishing*

Web: www.bookleafpub.com

E-mail: info@bookleafpub.com

ISBN: 9789363316720

First edition 2024

Every poem (if we can even call it that) has a song attached to it. (Well, some don't but they're not very enjoyable I'm afraid.) So I'd like to thank the artists/bands: Guns n Roses, Cat Pierce, Arctic Monkeys, Radiohead, Quavo & Lana Del Ray, Apparat, Tame Impala, Cigarettes After Sex, Rage Against the Machine, NF, Darci, Clams Casino & Imogen Heap, The Verve, MGMT, Peter Gabriel, Teho Teardo & Blixa Bargeld, Agnes Obel, Andrew Bird, Beach House, Tom Odell, Fall Out BoyAlt-J, Soap&Skin, and Ghost.

I also want to thank Douglas Adams because I borrowed Deep Thought's story for a poem.

Last but not least, I wanna thank me. I wanna thank me for showing up and following through. If you don't know me, this is a big (excuse my language) fucking deal to me.

ACKNOWLEDGEMENT

Thank you, Shivam. If not for you, I'd have never written a word again.

To my best friends, Meghna and Vinayak (in no particular order, so please don't fight), I am here because of you. Your friendship means more than my puny words can convey. I hope you feel my warmth from afar.

To Arpit, I'm sorry I didn't realize your light was going out. You were there for me, and I couldn't convince you to hold on. And thank you for existing. Until we meet again.

To my parents, I am grateful to you. Even if I might not always show it.

To all my dogs and all the dogs on this planet, you're a good boy/girl! I live for your wide grins.

PREFACE

Why does anyone do anything? A broken heart is the best catalyst for art.

Not that any of my work is great, but this process has been cathartic. I'm not a poet and I know it. But if you do decide to read this and relate to it, here's a virtual hug, friend.

The poems are out of order, so flip to any page at random. There's a recommended song attached to almost every poem that you could listen to enhance the experience. Or you could just listen to the song and toss the book away. Your call.

The themes are pretty dark, so proceed with caution. And if you don't know me, well, now you do :)

Go/Stay

Best enjoyed with November Rain by Guns n Roses

"Don't sleep. Not yet."
So I lay in wait with bated breath.

One by one, everyone else embraced death's
cousin.

So he wrapped his arms around me
Squished my face like he always would
When no one was watching.

Drew near and whispered the words I'd longed
to hear
But when he withdrew, in his eyes, I saw the
depths of his despair
For when he said "Go," he meant "Stay."

He thought I'd behave.
But "nothing lasts forever.
And we both know hearts can change."

Viraha

Best enjoyed with You Belong To Me by Cat
Pierce

In a parallel universe, you keep your word and
show up.
We watch that horror movie we said we would,
and I keep you up all night.
Picking apart the scenes, of course ;) The
allegory. The propaganda…
And you silence me the best way you know how.

You kiss me like a man just outta prison.
I kiss you back and finally
Finally, I feel I'm home.

The whole "right person, wrong time" is true.
And so is every darn person who told me I'd act
like a fool
Because my brain starts churning out scenes of
domestic bliss.
Fully believing this
This fever dream.

In a parallel universe, I know the right thing to
say so you never go back on your word,
Because in this one…

I don't.

P.S. Your anger never scared me because rage
has followed me like a stalker most of my life
too.

If sunshine were a person, it would be you

Best enjoyed with Tough by Quavo & Lana Del Ray

If I said I didn't know love, it'd be a lie.
Because you loved me even when it'd terrify

Most people.

To see the rot within,
The darkness that crept in,
The demons that'd never let me be.

And you sat there looking at me like I was
beautiful
Painstakingly picking out every burr from my
soul
Instead of throwing platitudes in my face.

Have I been half as good to you?
I always feel like I take more than I give.

I'm learning. I promise.

For all the wonderful things I've seen in this life,
The best thing about it is you.

I found God

Best enjoyed with Goodbye by Apparat

I would give anything to have Clementine's
balls.
But to erase you would be to erase me.
Because before you, I had no idea how anyone
falls
In love so deep they don't even realize it.

I carried the weight of these feelings around for
a long time
Well before I even became aware of them.
But I bricked up those feelings because you
weren't mine,
And I would never try to get in the way of your
happiness.

So when you finally took my hand in yours,
telling me it was over,
My dams burst.
I allowed myself to hope.
And that was my only mistake.

Because the day you were meant to return,
I dreamt a terrible dream —
You spoke of another.

But the truth was far more sinister.

Your conscience bogged down by misplaced
guilt,
You wanted to spare me the pain.

And I don't know how to tell you that I had to
go down on my knees,
Begging every God in existence
Any God that'd listen
To steal away my pain.

This book, this whole fucking experience,
Is your gift. If I hadn't felt this pain,
I would've never written a word again.

Feels like murder

Best enjoyed with Eventually by Tame Impala

Our imperfect love deserved a second chance.
But I was tired of fighting.

So I lay down my arms and curled up next to
you one last time,
Through the large French doors, I looked at the
vast sky outside.

I'd never seen the sky look that way—
Hues of purple and blue.

I knew then it was over,
Not because you said it was,
But because when we met, the sky was two
lovers tangled
Up in each other.
And now it looked like someone being slowly
strangled.

The other woman

Best enjoyed with Affection by Cigarettes after sex

I wish that we'd never seen each other again.
Because I'm always going to hold it against the
first perfect night.
And it's never going to be that perfect again.

But how lovely it is to get to know someone so
in love with themselves.
So sure of what they want.

I'm not sure what it was but I looked at you and
just smiled and your face broke into a grin and
for a split second I was just...happy.

I keep biting my tongue around you. I want to
say so much but I would rather listen.

I'm looking for a concrete flaw.
Something that I can make a mental note of.
Something that will stop me from getting
attached to you.

And so far, I have nothing.

But you wondered out loud
if you'd ever fall in love again.
And then it hit me…
"Of course, I'm the rebound."

Today, my ex texted me.
A seemingly innocent text and I saw his new
profile picture.
With his new girlfriend.
His college-aged girlfriend.

And for 5 seconds, I found it hard to breathe.
But then, I had another sinking feeling.

I am never going to know what it feels like to be
loved again.

Always the other woman, never the girlfriend.
I wish I could play the game.

I promised myself that I'd never let myself get
hurt again.
But this feels a lot like pain. Everything I don't
say to you weighs on my chest.

I don't want to get used to you or anyone. I don't
want to feel anything. But I can't deny that I do.
I'm happy when you're around.

I feel like I'm listening to an older version of me.
You are everything I could be.

Despite all that shit that I went through, I could
be happy.

Rage against the machine

Best enjoyed with Killing in the name of by
Rage Against the Machine

The PA system buzzed
To announce a moment of silence for a colleague
He was so young. Had so much life left in him.

But as soon as the moment was over
People broke out in chatter
Someone cracked a joke
And there was laughter.

I became numb.
Staring at this computer screen.
The numbers started swimming
I swear they turned to Matrix green
Falling like rain.

But I'm human too.
So on I went with my life.
I'd stare at the ceiling
And eat my feelings
Out of cardboard boxes
Sat in front of yet another screen
Consuming ungodly amounts of brain-dead TV.

"It could be worse," they say.

Lies.

It's how they keep us hooked.

"All companies work this way,"

Cries the HR when I ask for a day off.

"My friend died by suicide," I murmur.

"Okay, well, as long as you respect the dead lines."

But you won't respect the dead?

I will not die for your company.
I will not be told that rest is a privilege.
I will not be a cog in your wheel.
I will rage rage rage against the machine.

No Freaky Friday

Best enjoyed with Hope by NF

Talking about my body like I'm a collection of
parts
Forcing all this blame
And unsolicited advice down my throat
My unwieldy frame
Is picked apart.

Oh I'd swap places with you
Wake up with the first ray of the sun
Wear a smile
Get things done

On autopilot
Like you seem to.

But you
You wouldn't survive a day in my head

You never had to reason with yourself
To live another five minutes.
Then another five.
And another five.

You never had to reason with yourself

To slowly drop
The knife and back away.

You never had to tell the unkind voices in your head
To stop.

And if you did…
If you hate me because you see you in me,
I'm sorry.
The world's a cold place.
I'm glad you could white-knuckle through your pain
But you and I are not the same.

We live in time

Best enjoyed with On My Own by Darci

Can I see you again?
I'd like to see if you are as you were.

Did the cold world change you?
Like it did me?

Do you still fight the good fight?
Does your nose still crinkle when you laugh?
Do your nightmares still haunt you in the
daytime?
Does your lover know?

People are like time capsules.
Meeting you will be like meeting an old
friend—
Another version of me
That lived and died.

Bite Tongue, Deep Breaths

"I'm not beautiful.
My eyes aren't bright.
My eyebrows aren't right.
My haircut is awful."

My baby sister whined.
I told her she was perfect.

That everyone is.

I don't think she believed me.
She could see I didn't quite believe it myself.

But I didn't have the heart to tell her that I did
Once, many moons ago, I did.
I believed.

But I trusted too quick
My innocence sullied
By the lust of men
I should have studied
What happens after

Because I treated me the same as they did.

The meaning

***Best enjoyed with Bittersweet Symphony by
The Verve***

"The answer to the ultimate question
To life, the universe and everything…" said
Deep Thought

The intelligent beings fell silent.
So quiet you could hear a mosquito's finest
symphony.

"….is 42."
"42?!"

"Whatever does that mean?" pleaded the crowd.
"The answer will only make sense if you have
the ultimate question," Deep Thought rumbled.

"And what is the ultimate question?"
But Deep Thought didn't know.
It needed another computer.
One it would design
Where human beings would take more primitive
forms
And go through the motions for 10 million
years.

In search of the ULTIMATE QUESTION.

I hate to break it to you.
But the program failed.
The Gods went away.
We could never rise above our base instincts
Our reptilian brain.

We were meant to journey inward
But we landed on Mars instead.
Nothing wrong with reaching for the stars
After all, we're the same.

But the quest for purpose is now a privilege
The hungry crave a morsel
The war-torn crave rest
The beaten crave respite
And the rest of us, mortals, are living for a bite.

A bite of success, a whiff of freedom
Whatever that really means.

The pit

***Best enjoyed with How to Disappear
Completely by Radiohead***

No, that's okay.
I'm not like most people.
But some days,
I like to pretend.

My deep-seated need
For external validation
Is a product of neglect and conditioning.

Maybe I don't need it at all.
I've survived this long.

But sometimes, I yearn
For a place I can call home —
The arms of a lover, perhaps.

But I'm selfish because I have nothing to offer
I'm no haven.
I'm drowning.

No one should have to risk their sanity to pull
me out.

But I still hope that someone will be insane
enough to try.

Because if I could see the light at the end of the
tunnel,
I'd pull myself through.

I'd claw at the glass-like frictionless sides to
escape.
It'd take weeks,
Maybe months,
Maybe years.

But if I could see the light, I'd keep trying.

Until then,
The darkness comforts me.
It never leaves.
It's all I know.
It's here now.
I'll sleep.

Meat suit

I took on the pain and the punishment.
So you could live.

Free from the guilt and the blame.
While I had to relive
Those moments over and over and over and over
and over and over.

Won't you please ask them to lobotomize me?
I want to forget.

But the body keeps score.
Of what the mind forgets.

So, I find new ways to distract and sedate
You say this happened because it was fate
A past life, maybe?
Anything to shift the blame.

I'm tired, Mum.
Dad, I tried.

You didn't fail me.
But I can't toe the line.

Not anymore.

I died when I was nine.
I'm just dragging my meat suit to the finish line.

Chaotic evil

Best enjoyed with My Body is a Cage by Peter Gabriel

Chaos spills out my head
And into my room
I can't contain it anymore.

You're the reason I don't sleep
Without building a pile of my things
To guard me while I lay

I can't wish it away or ignore it
Like I do my reflection
A face I despise
Because I see faint traces of you in it.

I want it to stop.
I wish for a do-over.
But what if I wake up in another room?
Of your house

Wearing my pajamas
Rubbing my eyes
Sleep still in them
Clutching my hand-me-down bunny
Oblivious to the cycle of pain and horror

That awaits.

'Tis the season to introspect

***Best enjoyed with A Quiet Life by Teho Teardo
& Blixa Bargeld***

I'm ending this year, like most, a different
person.

It never gets easier when you realize a friendship
has run its course.
And if I may, this shit hurts more than a
heartbreak
For I've come to believe romantic love is
temporary.

Find a person you like to call your friend
And you begin to give and receive unconditional
love.
Hard to settle for anything less once you've
taken a hit of that.

So, we discard other people like chewed-up
gum.
Swimming in "endless" choices will do that to
you.
The first sign of trouble, and we bolt.

I know I'm guilty of doing that.

I'm trying to change.
But it's easier to cut people out than to be
vulnerable with them
Knowing full well they might break your heart
and you can't control it.

And that's something I've been obsessed with all
my life —
Control.

I never want to feel like the helpless child I was.
Again.
So I actively sought control.

But the only aspect of life
And perhaps the only aspect that counts —
human relationships — are beyond our control.

Accepting the mayfly nature of relationships can
help put things into perspective.
Maybe it's okay that our hearts break.
You have to destroy to create.

My Body is a Cage

Best enjoyed with It's Happening Again by Agnes Obel

The horror we imagine
Is worse
Than the horror
We witness.

Kinder than life

Best enjoyed with Three White Horses by Andrew Bird

When life flashes before my eyes
I wonder what I'll see.

Me chasing butterflies in the garden?
Whispered confessions?
The faces of my friends?

Will I see pain and agony?
Or is death kinder than life?

Will I see your eyes looking into mine?

Will I see my father taking me on a joyride?
Will I see my mother dancing in the rain with
me?

Will I hear my songs again?

Will I see the first time I saw snow?
The first time I saw a penguin slip?
Will a beautiful sunrise get a spot?
Or a lunar eclipse?

Will I remember the belly laughs?
All our shenanigans?
How food tasted so good
After a couple of hits?

Will I remember the vastness of the universe
And feel at ease knowing I'd be one again with
the stars?

Or will it cause anxiety?
Because I'm afraid of the unknown.

Will it feel like a second or an eternity?
Do you think I'll have time to rewind?

I do hope that death is kinder than life.

True Love Waits

***Best enjoyed with True Love Waits by
Radiohead or I wanna be yours by Arctic
Monkeys or Breezeblocks by Alt-J (pick your
poison)***

I love you so much
That I'd wash the dishes every night
And never complain.

I'd said I would never learn to cook
But for you, I'd suffer
Several rounds of being shook
And told, "You're an idiot sandwich."

Death metal isn't my jam,
But if you jumped in a mosh pit
I'd be right behind you.

At every party, I'd only have eyes for you.
And thank the angels up above
For sending me you.

Even though I hate not being in control,
I'd let you have the aux.
Would we finally find a new "our song"?

And when you'd grow weary and tired of life's
drivel,
I'd be your haven.
I'd sing you to sleep.
And then find my home again in your arms
While counting sheep.

I'd learn to drive.
I'd learn to thrive.
I'd learn to choose life.

I promise.

I love you so much
That I'd have your babies.

Maybe it's wrong to ask
But can I keep loving you from afar?

Quantum Immortality

Best enjoyed with Space Song by Beach House

A bed that gave me comfort
Now feels empty
Without your warmth in it.

I wish I hadn't fallen asleep so quickly
I wish I could take in every detail of your face
while you rested.

Never regretted almost failing in art
Until today
The way the moonlight hit your face and body
I wish I could transfer your beauty onto paper.

But maybe beauty isn't meant to be captured
It is to be enjoyed,
And consumed.

I wish I didn't feel this ache in my chest
Thought you wouldn't leave a you-shaped void
But waking up alone has never felt so lonely.

Can I sleep forever?
In my dreams, you don't hesitate.
In my dreams, you're all mine,

And I'm all yours.

If quantum immortality is a thing
I'll die in every timeline until I find one
Where you and I never left the room that night.

Speak

Best enjoyed in silence

Speak for the silenced.
Speak for the ones who don't even know what
freedom means.
Speak for the dead.
Speak for the ones who were trying to do the
right thing.
Speak for the innocent.
Speak for the children too young to know what
the monster in a human suit did.

If you have fingers, type.
If you have a conscience, fight.
Don't say this is just how life is.
"Boys will be boys" is an insult to all men.
Your daughters will hang their heads in shame.
Too afraid to be known by your name.

Vs.

The snake keeps eating its tail.
On the streets, we demand justice today.
But the status quo will remain.
Because you kill a man, not an idea.

If you chop Ravan's head off, another one
sprouts.
The seeds of supremacy, disdain, and abuse are
sown in childhood.
They want us to turn on each other.

Man vs. Woman.
Create religious divides.
Magnify cultural differences.
Use language as a weapon.
Blame the victim, not the perpetrators.
If we can't see through their lies, we'll be the
snake that eats its tail.

Never free

"78 years of freedom," they say.
What freedom is that?
Where I have to hide and cower
And I'm told to lower

My tone
My eyes
My stature

I bleed. They grope.
I plead. They poke.
I'm weak. I'm sure.

I should be happy it didn't go further
I should be happy they let me live
I should be happy I'm not in the papers
I must have invited the attention.
My clothes must have given them the wrong
idea.
My smile too wide. My laughter too loud.

It's my fault. I left the house.
It's my fault. I was in school.
It's my fault. I was roofied.
It's my fault. I was at home.
It's my fault. I was with a friend.

It's my fault. I was with a boyfriend.
It's my fault. I was at the train station.
It's my fault. I was standing on the pavement.
It's my fault. I was on a date.
It's my fault. My friend was running late.

Promise me you'll burn my body the second it
turns cold.
Don't wait hours for the funeral.
Promise me you won't let my corpse out of your
sight.
Don't let them touch me. You'll know how I
died.
And if I come back to this earth again,
Please send me back if I'm born a woman.

Minus love

Best enjoyed with Daydreaming by Radiohead

And suddenly, I didn't care about love
I just wanted my head to stop swimming.

Love didn't feel essential.
I just wanted to breathe without struggling.

Love felt like a pipe dream.
I just wanted to eat again and have food taste the
same.

Love didn't feel like the oxygen I needed to
survive.
I just wanted to be able to sleep again.

You can go away now.
I've learned what's more important.
And no, it's not love. It was never love.

In too deep

Best enjoyed with New Person, Same Old Mistakes by Tame Impala

He makes me feel beautiful
And he's never even seen anything but my face

Maybe one day he will
Maybe one day he will see the ugliness.

But he knows
He knows the things I've left unsaid
He knows my heart better than most

His words soothe my brain
His velvety voice wraps itself around me like a hug
His eyes. I could look into those eyes forever.
I'm drowning but I don't care.

I want his arms around me
His whispers in my ears
I want him to take what he needs
And give me all that he is
I want a part of him
I want to give him a part of me
So he carries me with him

And I'll carry him with me.

Some things last

Best enjoyed with Heal by Tom Odell

The air is stale.
My breath is stuck.
The plants are dead.

But I keep looking at the door.
The door opens
Someone's ushered in.

I don't know when it'll be my turn
I've been counting tiles on the floor
Tracing the cracks in the wall

Some kid is going off like a whistle
I tell myself I won't stick around all day
My to-do list is as long as all the things I regret

I can't wait for him to tell me there's something
wrong with my brain.
Maybe it's nothing.
But I imagine what it'd be like to forget.

To forget the pain
To forget how the rain
Smells

To forget everything
To forget you

But I don't think I could forget you
I may not recognize my face one day
But yours?
Yours is burned in my brain.

Nightmares

It's been years
But you haunt me in my dreams.

My brain's convinced you're in the room.
My dream's so vivid
I can't tell the difference.

And if how we perceive reality is decided by our minds
Then I'm reliving the nightmare again
And again.
You win.

I was six.
The first time it happened.
I was six.

I don't know what's sadder
The words "the first time"
Or "I was six"

I didn't even know what was happening
I just knew it wasn't right

Maybe he didn't know either
But he did it anyway

And left me with a lifetime of pain
While he escaped unscathed.

And men wonder why we choose the bear
Dying once is better than dying every day.

8 minutes

It's like fighting with a goldfish.
You don't remember my trauma.

But do you remember
How I became withdrawn?
How I stopped smiling?
How I'd spend all my time reading?
The suicide letters I wrote?
How I cried till I couldn't breathe?

It isn't your fault. Or mine.
But you missed all the signs.
And now you don't even remember my
adolescence
Or how I tried to end it.

A part of me will never understand.
But I forgive you and him.
Because that rage is boiling me alive
Not you or him.

The Demon is me

Best enjoyed with Cirice by Ghost

I look down at my hands
And suddenly I'm seeing double.

Are these mine?
My face?
My voice?
Who is this?
Me?
Am I really here?

I have this odd sensation that I'm being watched
But not by another
I feel I'm watching myself
Almost like in a movie
Then I'm suddenly scared.

My tears won't stop rolling down.
And through the tears, I start laughing.

Laughing at the ridiculousness of it all.
Laughing at the meaningless suffering
Laughing at my meat suit
And something dark slips through.

I fear I'm a demon.
Only that could explain my suffering.

Untouched

There's nothing to enjoy about this one. My apologies.

I couldn't sit at the altar and pretend
Good always wins
So why had my God failed?
Why did He let that happen?
Not once, not twice, but for three thousand and
sixty-five
Days that I counted

I counted sheep
I counted the tiles in the ceiling.
I counted my breaths.

But I lost count of the days
And I'd wake up screaming.

I had a bad dream.
It was happening all over again.
And some days, I didn't need to be asleep.
To feel your hands over me.

I wanted to walk into a shredder
I wanted to skin myself alive
I wanted a new body
Untouched and unsullied.

I still don't want to be here

"I don't want to be here."
I wrote.

But I'm scared my mum won't be able to cope.
My dad will live. He's stronger than most.
But I don't want to be here.

"Why sweetheart?"
My grandfather asked.

"I don't know, Pops."

But now I know.
The body keeps score of what the mind tries to
forget.

I was wasting away, rotten to the core.
I was only nine years old.

Hello sinner

You won't enjoy this one either. But listen to
Me and the Devil by Soap&Skin

I was six.
And in some ways, I still am.

I'm sure you did it for the cheap thrills.
I'm sure you don't even remember the pink
Bows I used to tie in my hair.

I didn't even know what was happening.
Did you?
When they beat the truth out of you,
You said his older brother told you to do it.

Why?
Because she's cute.
I didn't hear what was said after.

And that was when I started despising my face.
Cute = danger
Seared into my memory.

But the worst thing I remember wasn't what you
did to me
It was a woman.

A teacher.
My teacher.
Who cornered me and asked if I had a tongue in
my mouth
Couldn't I speak?

I didn't say anything to her then.
Remember, I was only six.

But I'd like to dance on her grave.

And when your time comes,
I hope you see my face.

9 789363 316720